TO WHOM IT MAY CONCERN:

A Poetry Collection

Written by
Nytesia Ross

For you, for me, or for someone else entirely...

Contents

HEALING

Story.

When you open yourself like a book, people will read you.
They will determine the best and worst parts of what they've read.
They will judge whether your mistakes are redeemable
Whether you're worthy of them going page by page
   to see your progression.
Some may close the book halfway through, some may read till the
   very end, and some may put you back on the shelf.
But regardless of what readers may do
   You are still a story worth being told.

We let them.

Why do we make what others say about us an unbreakable law?
Giving them power to deem beauty as flaw.

Curiosity.

Will you be the sculptor of your own life?
Or are your dreams in another potter's hands?

Blank Canvas.

What a shame it would be to become what
  someone else envisions.

Question.

Am I still a masterpiece after rips and tears...?
... after the handler stores me away.
Am I still a masterpiece or am I just... pieces
  of something unknown?

Acknowledgement.

Daddy issues—become my issues.
His inability to stay—my inability to leave the past alone.
Trying to focus on the love that I receive
Instead of using all of my energy to prove that I am worth loving.

I have questions!
Why is it so hard for you to love me?
... to see me as your own.
I am part of you.
How come my soul seems to be tied to you but yours not to mine?
Wondering if a man can love me when my own blood could not
    love me first.
I'm sad and misunderstood.

My choices, at least some of them have been influenced by you.
Success was never an option—I had something to prove.
Waiting on that congratulatory speech you would give me... when
    trying to make an introduction into my life.
Telling myself *I must succeed!*
The day must come... when I can say, "I did it without you!"

I stop myself.

This is not your father's life.
This is yours.
Do not be fueled by his absence.
Do not aspire to gloat in his presence.
You have questions as to why he was absent
Well, here it is.
His purpose was to help create you.
That's it.
And that's what he did.

Well, how about that, "father?"
I guess it is a job well done.

Lesson from my father.

I realized that my father ain't the only one who had a problem
   with loving something so precious.
It somehow trickled down to me.

I ain't always gave that girl in the mirror the loving she needs.
Nor the attention she needs.

I gave it all to someone else.

My father ain't teach me nothing but how not to love myself.

Reality.

At times I feel broken, helpless.
I have no control—no say.
I'm drowning in expectations.
I cannot breathe.
I can't breathe.
I'm trying to find myself.
But I fear I am out of my depth.

False Statements.

Broken is a word meant for something that needs fixing.
You do not need fixing.
You are tired.
You are hurt.
You are many things.
But broken—you are not.

Vulnerable.

Death was an option for me.
Escaping what is, the complications of my reality.
People think the thought comes easy
... as if you don't have the desire to live
but some things aren't that simple.
Sometimes you just don't want to hurt.
You want the pain to subside.
You want something definite.
Something that you feel you have control over because
    control is what you're lacking
... and the finality of death is appealing.
See, some know this feeling.
And thankfully some don't.
But to those who do, and who are reading this...
Know that you are HUMAN, and you are ALIVE.
And you are NEEDED.
So keep breathing.
Keep living.
And know that YOU are not alone.

You're here for a reason.

Do me a favor.
Take a deep breath.
Put your hand on your chest.
Focus on the words that you are reading.
Say the next sentences aloud.
"I am enough.
I am enough.
It is me and God.
I take ownership of what God has given me.
My joy, my peace, my love and anything that has been stolen... is back
  in my possession.
It is mine."
Now check your pulse.

Remember to...

Cherish the moments when laughter comes effortlessly.
When you look around and realize you're surrounded
   by only love.
When the sun is shining and you feel you are too.
When your worries have settled and peace becomes
   overwhelming...
I pray you smile.
Breathe in and out.
Because though the world has tried to steal your joy... you
   are still standing.
You are still here.

Letting go.

When you forgive someone, must they know?
Is there a conversation that happens between you both or is the
   convo between you and growth?

And what does forgiveness look like?
Does it look like everything before the pain and the betrayal?
Is it back to normal or is it something new?
Does "new" even exist?
Is it a phone call or a holiday text?
Or is it an unsaved number?

How does the heart feel through it all?
Does it race, does it beat at a steady pace?
Does the wall it's enclosed in come down?
Or does it stay up?

Maybe forgiveness is understanding.
That you—are not me.
You move differently—for reasons that I am not privy to.
Maybe it's me—accepting the fact that you are in fact human.

Or maybe forgiveness is for me.
To not allow the loving parts of me to be tainted by the ugly parts
   of you—in which you've shown.

A letter to my future self.

Today, I woke up and I put us first... for the very first time.
It was much harder than I expected, but it was needed.

I did it because I didn't want to disappoint us.
I didn't want us to look back and say "why didn't we fight
   to love us?"
Why was "our well-being" at the bottom of our priority list?
Why didn't we tend to the pieces of ourselves that
   needed healing?—
Giving ourselves away to everyone and everything but not once
   giving ourself attention.

Nytesia, I want you to know that if no one loves you... I do.
I did.
I will.
I started today.

To whom it may concern,

Looking in the mirror will not always be your favorite thing to do—
    but you should do it.
Why?
Because you should always be able to look at yourself.

There should be times you look and see that nothing needs fixing.
No contour, no shaving, just you.

There should be times you take one picture and post it.
Don't think too hard.
Don't add a filter.
You are enough.
One picture is enough.

He or she may not see you.
They might overlook your love while they seek what you have
    inside of you, inside of someone else.
It is okay.
At one point you too didn't value what was in front of you.

The grass may very well be greener on the other side.
But that's none of your concern.
Find out which fertilizer works best for your yard—the Son will
    shine on it in its time.

In due time, clarity will come. Or maybe it won't.
You'll have to figure out how to deal with it.

Childhood trauma needs to be addressed; generational curses
    need to be broken.
Face it—head on.

Watch out for following societal rules.
What a shame it would be if the world never got to
  know the real you.
If you never got to know the real you.
Don't be ashamed of your hair, your ethnicity,
  or dwell on mistakes that taught you something.

Remember life is chaotic, never going as planned,
  never exactly what you expect.
But don't waver.

Always speak up for what's right.
Your knees may shake,
Your voice may quiver,
But you got this!
I wouldn't say it if it wasn't true.

Therapy.

Healing can come by confronting truth.
But can't nothing be done, can't nothing be fixed, if you fail to
  reflect and address it.

Looking Back.

Your past may be a place you visit but you must not stay.

HOME

What is home?

Household be teaching ground... be battlefield... be safe haven...
   be danger zone... for some.

It be bad memories... negative vibes... where you get whuppings
   when you cry.
Never mentioning the pain that entered the doorway and never
   left... when the closest you get to escaping is the doorway steps.

It be a place where generational curses be prayed and oiled out.
Where manners are taught... "yes mam"... "no sir"... look people
   in their eyes when you talk.

Where a child had to grow up too fast... be the adult... be the
   protector... and the provider.

Where dreams were formed, and dreams were crushed.
Where food was low, but bellies were full.
Where toys were few, but rent was paid.

Where imaginary friends came in handy during hard times.
Where a pillow muffled the sound of a heart-wrenching cry.

Where the silver spoon was always clean.
And Nanny took care of the important things.

Where mom was gone, and father was busy, but money was
   always plenty.

Where love was present, and conversations were had.
Where lessons were taught with grace and hugs were
   given when sad.

Household be teaching ground... be battlefield... be safe haven...
   be danger zone... for some.

The start of the week.

Momma cleans on Sundays.
She really cleans throughout the week—call it therapy.
But Sundays hit different.
The blinds come up—
The music come on—
We're listening to gospel or blues depending on her mood.
She mixes that soap and that water,
And starts mopping the kitchen floor.
In the bedroom,
She brings the broom—
And starts dancing with it.
Singing—as if it's one of the gifts God gave her.
The house smells like Clorox and a scented candle.
Sundays become the days we start putting the pieces
    back together.
Momma say, "ain't nothing like a clean house to make you
    feel a little better!"

Refreshing.

I sit in the bathtub in my first apartment,
I place my middle finger on my right thigh...
...rub it against my brown skin.
I then take my towel and soap and begin washing my body clean
   of the day.
I watch as the water darkens.
I am sitting in today's sins.
I stand up after washing myself clean... and smile...
   for I am still whole.
I am still intact.

Ownership.

You are here... in this space.
This is your space.
Your land.
Your home.
Your body.
This is yours.
Be you.
Be true.
And stand.
Stand up, this is home!
Protect home.

Safe Haven.

There's nothing but open space, to think, to feel, to love, to hate,
    to explore infinite possibilities.
This is fantasy mixed with reality.

I am comfortable.
I am learning more about myself.
I am able to be myself.
Others are welcome to join.
Places like these allow for reflection and candor.

A snow globe is sitting comfortably to my right.
It is a constant reminder of beauty and how change only comes
    when you decide to do something different.
When you decide to shake things up.

Pictures are protected by frames that hold memories of different
    moments shared with loved ones and friends.

This is my temple.
It is sacred.
I have cried tears and shared my inner truth within these walls.

At 6 a.m., sunlight presents itself as an enemy.
It watches over me, it whispers, "it's time."

I get myself ready; it's time to go, it's time to leave my sanctuary.

Where is home?

I'll never forget the time I saw a sea lion and a dolphin
    in an enclosure.
They looked happy, they looked friendly... but they
    were confined.

They did tricks, danced, and took pics in exchange for fish.
But I couldn't help but notice—scratches on their bodies and
    wondered how they got there.
I was told that the dolphins fight one another, and the sea lions
    scratch themselves.
And that may be true.
but I kept wondering... should they be caged?

Is it natural... is it right... to take them from their habitat to be
    entertainment for those who pay to see?
An instructor told me that they sometimes have to force the sea
    lion to go out to sea.
Which made me wonder how long it takes a sea lion to forget that
    sea is home... that predator includes humans?—that this
    familiar place limits their freedom.
That some of their sisters and brothers are living a life they'll
    never get to see.

Wonder Thoughts.

When I look out my window, I see a tree; I gaze at its trunk and
    begin to think about what causes tree limbs to bend... to
    break... or an entire tree to fall.
I believe the elements play a part.
        When Earth says, "your time is up."
The Wind comes, breaks you into pieces.
An abundance of Water comes, making it hard to breathe.
And Fire burns you down.

Though rooted in the Earth,
susceptible to destruction.
Beautiful when left alone, but deadly when swept up by tornado.
A source of oxygen.
A piece of decoration.
Trees be many things, just as we.

You leave better. I'm still stuck.

They wonder how a spirit so pure could leave, without warning.

They forget that "heavy" is a thing.
That "I'm okay" is not always reality.
That baggage is sometimes not your own
It's others who have dropped their pain at your doorstep, not
    knowing your house is already filled with bags of your own.

When you're dealing with confusion, depression, and demons
    that refuse to leave, though the door is open
Folks mistake it for an entry way instead of an exit.
House be a place for everyone else to have their therapy session.

They don't notice this place is standing on its last two legs.
They only see the eviction sign when spirit leaves.
No one bothered to take care of the person they deemed
    a sanctuary.

Dead with a pulse.

Deathbeds don't always see the dying.
They see the ones who have breath but don't appreciate it.
Those who don't see the opportunity in the day
who just sit in a sea of their own complaints.

Wisdom.

It's Wednesday, and I'm sitting on the couch, on the phone
    with my Granny.
We talk about this and that, and I acknowledge we are halfway
    through the week.

I then say, "I'm just ready to get to Friday."

Granny replies, "T, be careful with wishing your days away."

I pause to process.

Because Granny is right—by no surprise.
I realize, that's what I'm doing—disregarding the blessing of the
    current day while eagerly awaiting another.
Ready to fast forward—when truthfully, I don't know what Friday
    may bring—what it may have in store.

But what I do know, is God has given me Wednesday.
So, I won't dare wish my day away.

What is life?

Life happens fast.
The Bible says, "Life is but a vapor that appeareth for a little time
and then vanishes away."
In an instant things can change.
Body be in ground and mourning begins.
Mobility be taken and mind forgets.
Days come and go.
Moments be captured in video.
Milestones be captured in photographs.
As we recycle conversations about the past.
But what about today?
Though rainy, breath still be in body, faith still be in God.
So today I'll live.
Fearlessly.
For this life is not long.
It is but "a vapor that appeareth for a little time... and then
vanishes away."

James 4:14

Let's Live.

Get the dominos.

Get the folding table.

Turn on some blues.

You know them 2's be spades too.

Got Crown in hand.

Juice boxes for the kids.

Uncles washing the cars,
While momma and granny cookin.

Good conversations
And jokes and praise–

Nothing beats the good ole days.

Nostalgia.

Laying in my bed—reminiscing.
Thinking—once upon a time,
We did flash mobs
And mannequin challenges.

We spray-painted our shirts and headbands with our names.
We decorated our Game Boy's with stickers.
Bejeweled was all the rage.
So was Diner Dash and the Sims—
And Pokémon cards.

And you can't forget that
Raven was seeing the future,
Brandy lost her glass slipper,
Lindsay was in the parent trap,
And Anne was princess of Genovia.

We were also trying to find Nemo,
Moving like Dora the Explorer with only Blue's Clues,
But we were solving problems like Jimmy Neutron,
And ended up digging a few Holes of our own, while dressed like
    SpongeBob with those SquarePants,
See we were really just a bunch of Rugrats, with Fairly
    Odd Parents.

Nonetheless,

So much was happening on our screens.
We had flip phones, iPods and DVDs.
We were passing notes—do you like me? Yes or no?
Kids were jumping on trampolines
Listening to the radio.

Waiting for AOL dial up
And calling folks on 3 way
Playing like we answered the phone
    but folks was really talking to our voicemails
We put beads at the ends of our ponytails
We made those boondoggle bracelets
and we were selling them...
To buy them—big lollipops, gushers,
sour skittles, or hubba bubba bubble tape
Or maybe those mood rings, ankle skip balls,
    spin tops, bop it, or beyblades.

People was at 106 & Park and getting punked on TV.
We were punching the air... playing the Wii.

We messed with Lava lamps, Snake, and Tetris
We listened to the jingle from education connection

Now I know I'm being nostalgic,
But my gosh, these things happened,
Once upon a time.

Forward.

Though I don't know what lies ahead
I hope I find my way... to my destined place
Where my mind, body, heart, and soul can safely dwell.

HER

Creator's Creation.

There is nothing more beautiful in this world than she.
Her spine don't bend.
Her love ain't nothing to be played with.
Her life be a testament.
Her body be a temple.
Sadly, places like these, people tend to mistreat.
They forget this body is immaculate.
That this stomach may be home for somebody.
These arms be a resting place for the man who is tired, the child
    who is crying, and for herself…
… after she is done carrying the weight of everyone else.
Woman be biblical.
Praying as Hannah.
Loyal as Ruth.
Birthing or caring for greatness like Mary.
She is setting the table.
Cooking the food.
Bringing home money.
And fighting for equality too.
She is holding CEO positions.
When she speaks, you should listen.
She is serving her community.
She is whomever she chooses to be.
She is everything!
She is resilient.
She is strength.
Even when her body tries to betray her.
For some days aren't always the best but she fights.
For life.
Walking to the beat of her own drum.
She is poetry.
She is song.
And again, I say, "there ain't nothing more beautiful than she.
For SHE is woman."

A Woman.

Formed from the rib of Adam
Taken from his side so she would never be mistaken for anything
  less than his equal.
But as time goes on, she has been pressured to believe that
  standing by his side is not exactly her position.
She is told that a man is to be superior—over his woman.
That woman would be nothing without man.
But this point is not valid, for anything that's valid needs proof.

And in a book that holds many stories about this life that we live.
A book that tells us our creator is the orchestrator of the universe.
A book that does not lie.
A book that's not a fairytale yet holds the meaning of life.
This same book tells us in 1 Corinthians 11:9 that "woman was
  made for man."
"For it was not good for man to be alone," so God created us.
— Genesis 2:18.

And yes, some men believe they don't need us.
And yes, some women believe men don't need us.
But this is simply not true.
For God knew in a man's heart he would feel empty.
Never would he feel complete.
Tears flowing from his eyes because he would never understand
  where the void he feels comes from... when it ultimately comes
  from the absence of a woman.

A woman, the caretaker of her family.
She wipes away the tears of her young one's eyes and whispers
wisdom in their ear.
She picks her man up when he's at his lowest and carries some of
the weight when needed.
She is the one her family can count on... the chosen shoulder to
cry on.
She has an extraordinary gift.
To lessen the pain when at times life can seem unbearable.
What she can do is extremely admirable.

A woman is strong.
Being able to withstand excruciating pain through the only outlet
God made for humanity to enter into this world.
She is a glorified creation.
She is the way Jesus came. Jesus—the giver of our salvation.

A woman should never be called out of her name nor mistreated
or misused.
She should be treated like royalty... for her Father is a King... for
He states that her price is "far above rubies... her tongue is the
law of kindness and does not eat the bread of idleness."

This same woman who is stated in Proverbs 31, is predestined to
prevail through any obstacles she may face— for this I know
is true.
For God said, it wasn't good for man to be alone, so He
created you.

Beloved.

You have a responsibility: to NEVER underestimate your being.

Let's talk about it.

I've seen Black Woman tend to everyone else's wounds and then
  fix her eyes on her own.

Black Woman is who some run from—but all cry to.
Her arms be a place you eventually seek refuge.
She loves and protects you.

When you ask who knows, she knows—the recipe, the remedy
a problem solver, she tends to be.
She's the ally that you seek.
The superhero you do not recognize her to be.

You know.

You treat us like saviors
Ones who swoop in and make everything right.
It's probably because of the Black woman who in her own way
   tucked you in at night.

Between grandma, momma, auntie, sister, and little girl you're
   dating down the street, you're protected.

From one of them you're getting guidance, they're keeping you
   up on game.
In another you are running into their arms—unloading
   all of your pain.
All of 'em ready to fight for you, go to war behind your name.
Yet the echoes for her are rarely the same.

Why does a Black woman have to fight so hard for her existence?
Why is her voice not heard, neither at home, or workplace, or in
   the ground?—only when she is soothing fragile egos?

Tell Me.

Where are the search parties?
Where are the folks knocking on doors and signing petitions for
 the Black girls?

For the Black girls taken, for the Black girls detained, for the
 Black girls whom we still don't know their names.

Where's the fight for the Black girls?

Who's fighting for the Black girls?
Who's protecting the Black girls?
Who's praying for the Black girls?

The Black girls?!

What do you see?

When I see a Black woman I see strong
By force and by nature.
When I see a Black woman I see healer
Both physical and mental.

Patching up old wounds... new wounds...
Neglecting her wounds... for their wounds.

The Black belly is the money womb.
From cotton pick or the draft pick, she produces it.

Expectancy.

Why Black women got to be revolutionary all the got dang time!?
Can we just be?
Can't folk just leave us be?

The J.O.B.

Best friend said she didn't want her hair to be the topic
    of conversation.
But we all knew it would be.
So here we are outside of a restaurant.
Discussing whether she should rock it straight or curly for
    the job interview.
You know why!
We all know why.
Long story short—she rocked it straight.
She got the job.

Listen here.

It's the blue magic for me.
It used to be the go-to for a scalp that needed to be greased.
Right before you go through with the hot comb
Sitting by its lonesome on the stove.
Ponytails with the barrettes and beads would follow.
Baby hairs slicked all the way back.
And that was just that.

Until we got to perms.
You couldn't scratch your head because you knew it would burn.
Trying to get that hair slick and straight
Until being introduced to the natural way.

Hair bending and molding.
The beauty of all the ways our hair can transform.
The space it commands.
The attention it draws.
The ruckus they say it causes
Our crowns deserve an applause
for it is art.
it is direction.
it is ours—to tell story,
To do with it as we please
It be our crowns for me.

Sis.

That puff on top of your head
those braids
those edges laid

You can rock it straight or curly
Micros or fro
Locs or bun on top
Rainbow colored or classic black
You can rock all of that!

Now, who's to tell a queen what to do with her crown?
Whether it be in the office or walking around town!?

If you said "no one" then you are correct.
It's no one's place to govern one's hair
Especially after the hours we spend in the salon chair.

Let me tell you something, Black Queen!
Your crown is beautiful!
It has always been.
You rock it well!
You rock it proud!
And anyone who has a problem, well they can move around!

Love Letter.

Black woman, this poem starts with you.

Inspiration is the Black woman I see in the kitchen—putting her
heart and soul into those homemade dishes.

It's the one who ain't got no kid of her own but is helping to raise
everyone else's.
She's a part of the community of women who makes sure you're
in church for those early Sunday School lessons.

She got as much education as she could.
She has two to three jobs to make sure the household good.

She's got diploma in hand.
She's degreed.
She's creating legacy down the street.

She's teacher, leader, builder.
She builds up children, men, and country.
With her wits—she keeps us fed with her signature grits.

She has no shame in luxury living,
For she earned it, she deserves it.

She brings her full self into every space,
Cuz bowing down is not an option.
Want to address her? Proceed with caution.
Cuz she be glorious, she got a divine covering.

Black woman, Oh, Black woman, this poem ends with you.

Woman to Woman.

To the Black woman who told Supreme Court Justice Ketanji
    Brown Jackson to "Persevere"
I want to say thank you.

Though your interaction was subtle and fleeting.
Your impact was not.

You saw her in a moment of question and doubt, and you sowed
    into her.
A word.
A reminder.
A push
To keep going
To persevere
And look at her now.

Promise me.

If you ever begin to doubt yourself
Remember that you add value to every space you enter.

You exemplify
Excellence, beauty, and grace.
You set the pace.

So, Sis!
Don't you dare shrink.
Whatever room you're in—you deserve to be.
Don't you dare question your abilities.
Set and protect your boundaries.

Send that email as is—don't you go back and forth in your mind
    press send!
Your tone is just fine.
Your ideas deserve airtime.

You got this.
I'm just here to remind you, Sis.

Thank You.

Sometimes you just need a Black woman
Yeah... you just need a Black woman
To lend her ears
To share her wisdom from throughout the years
To wipe your tears
To pray with
To plan with
To joke with
To laugh with
To encourage you to rest and relax.

Sometimes you just need a Black woman
To hold you
To show you
There is more
There is better for you.

Sometimes you just need a Black woman's guidance
When the lies try to stick
When the doubt starts creeping in
Sometimes you just need a Black woman to help you not get
    buried by the weight of the world, of family, of friends
A Black woman who will see you and help you up the mountain
    and hold your hand through the wilderness.

Sometimes you just need a Black woman—to say
Baby... or Sis!! Straighten your back.
Lift your head up.
Ain't nothing on the ground for you!
Seeds have already been sown
It's time for you to grow

To blossom
To bloom
You belong
Here.
Right here
In this role
In this position
In this space
You are qualified
You are gifted.
Sometimes you just need a Black woman to remind you that
You are exquisite.
That your greatness is something the ancestors would be proud
    to have witnessed.

You know...
Sometimes...
You just need a Black woman.

And oh... what it is to be a Black woman.
Black woman...

Rest.

Black woman, I need you to rest.
And I'm not talking about that quick little break you give
    yourself—I'm talking ceasing from action.
Meaning putting your superhero duties on pause
Giving yourself that long overdue applause
And someone else solving the problem.
I need you to just exist.
Put yourself at the top of your priority list
Responsibility will have to be someone else's.
I need you to focus on you
Your health, your wealth, yourself!

Don't Forget.

Black women ain't the only ones who be sewing.
That needle, that thread, be in Black men's hands too.
Piecing pieces back together... making anew.

Black Man.

I pray that when you need to cry—you do it.
And it's in a safe space.
And it's with people who dap you up and embrace you with love.

Black man, I pray that you give your body permission to move, to
    groove, and be held.
I pray that joy and laughter overwhelm you
And that worthy is how you see yourself.

Black man, I pray that when the weight is heavy, there is help
    around—and that each day there's a reason to smile.

Black man,
I pray you know that you're beautiful.
In every shade
In every way.

Powerful.

When I think of royalty
I don't think of gold crowns or elaborate robes.
I think of a body whose muscle memory does not know what
   bending over feels like.
I think of family ties that wouldn't dare be severed.
I think of water and wind being shut up in bones, producing
   movement as natural as the elements themselves.
I think of breath creating magnificent tones.
I think of a singular touch,
   where everything in reach turns to gold.
Black be regal, majestic, having history of spectacular opulence
Having a hand in innovation and creation.
Black be royalty.
Royalty be Black.

Representation.

We love to see it—Black children have Black Barbies and Black
    action figures to play with
They can set their eyes on Black medical illustrations.

They know of a Black Disney princess, a Black mermaid and a
    Black superhero.
They know of Black execs—CEOs

They'll learn about a Black President and VP
They can search Black billionaires and see Black love on tv

Black children have, know, and experience things
That for us were once, just a dream.

Real Talk.

Sometimes you can be Living Single,
In A Different World,
And That's So Raven.

And what a Smart Guy,
The Fresh Prince.
But sometimes you need a One on One
Cuz Everybody Hates Chris.

Or maybe it's Half & Half.
Like My Wife and Kids,
and they Girlfriends,
and they Sister, Sister.

But we really are The Proud Family.
aka The Parkers.
We got Moesha, Martin, Kenan and Kel, Jamie, Steve, Bernie,
    Malcolm and Eddie,
and best believe the Wayans Brothers always ready
To watch The Game.
We call this the House of Payne.
But listen, at the end of the day, Family Matters.

Young, Gifted, and Black.

To be young, gifted, and Black—my oh my.

To be young—is us.
Trying to figure this life thing out.
It ain't easy, it be challenging
We really hoping that everything works out.
Sometimes we put too much pressure on ourselves,
And there are times we don't put enough.
But hey, we're young!
We got ambition,
We got dreams,
And we're believing in God to do His thing.
To be young—and to make mistakes,
To be young—and to learn from them
Oh, to be young...

And to be gifted.
To have something inside of you that you can't fully comprehend.
Some things come so effortlessly.
Like pen to paper.
Keys to piano.
Voice to microphone.
Stage be home.
Because it was made for you.
In due time your gift will make room for you.
That's what God said, remember your life is in God's hands.
Oh, to be gifted is a gift!

To be Black.
Ain't nothing quite like it.
There's a freedom you have to find within yourself
But once you've found it—chains can't hold you back.
Heart be so big

Skin so beautiful
Moving to the tune of your own beat.
Holding true to what makes you happy

A Black boy smiling.
A Black girl resting.
A Black man in the comfort of his own
A Black woman unapologetically bold.

To be young, gifted, and Blackity, Black, Black, Black.
Now, ain't that something to be.
And that is what we are.
And I hope we don't forget it.

Honestly.

Have you ever heard a Black boy laugh?
It's beautiful.

Have you ever seen a Black girl dance?
It's magical.

Have you ever heard a Black man sing from the pits of his soul?
Have you ever looked at a Black woman and not questioned if
    she's whole?

There's so much more to Black stories than Black pain.
Like Black Joy and Black Praise.

Joy.

Black joy is a wide smile and a long embrace
It's hair free and untamed
It's deep breaths (pause)
It's a woosah and reset
It's giving each other compliments
It's dancing in the street to throwback songs
It's everybody getting in position for when them line dances
   come on
It's singing at the top of our lungs on key... off key
but together we gonna be moving in sync
Having a good time
Telling truth, telling lies
Speaking life
Bringing energy and light
Whether we frolicking in the park
Or double dutching in the dark, with nothing but the street
   lights on
This Black body is home
And nothing will interfere with joy residing here.

Black Praise.

I love Black folk.
I love when Black folk flood the dance floor when "before I let
    you go" comes on—pairing it with the electric slide, is the
    perfect recipe for a good time.
And let me tell you something!
Black folk know how to have a good time.

We be swaggin and surfin
And you better already know how to play spades
This ain't the time for learning.
Dominos and uno are sometimes the games of choice—bickering
    over the rules because sometimes we don't be on one accord.
"They put a draw 4, ima put a draw 2, and make you draw 6."
And to somebody that makes sense.

Did I mention I love us!?

The jokes—the sound that comes out of our mouths when
    we laugh
Paired with a knee slap—You know what I'm talking about.
The fashion—styling and profiling
Them big bright colored church hats.
The cooking—that sweet potato pie always slap.
Them prayers—made generations ago that's keeping us covered.
Them hymns—that we refer back to—lifting our voices over
    and over.

Our art, our music, our moves, our movies that we create.
And the change that we make.
The stories of our bodies.
The journey of our souls.
Black will always be home.

Did I mention I love us!?

Hey yall.

Cheers to Black existence,
Black resistance
And Black persistence.

Black resilience
And Black brilliance,

Taking up space
Moving with grace
Our healing and beauty we celebrate.
Not just today but every day.

HISTORY

The land of...

They say America be home to people
Be both sanctuary and safe haven.
They say America be death angel...
Both torturous and evil.

You see, America is whatever people
     who take up its name want it to be.
Its history is long.
It is both heartbreaking and victorious
Depending on who you ask.

It is where human rights have not always been right
     for certain people.
It is where people have stolen land... taken it up as their own and
     slaughtered those to whom it truly belongs.

America for some is a symbol of refuge
It is a place for a better life.
It is a melting pot... a magnificent taste
but some choose not to be served a plate
Not everyone's palate is the same.

They say America is a place of dreams.
It is a place of opportunity.
It is a place where the people decide...
Destruction or progression.
Division or unification.
So, what kind of nation is it and
what kind of nation will it become?
Will America be more than the pain it knows,
     it shows, it grows?
Will it be what it has always been or something different?

History.

When you don't learn—when you're not taught historical truth
  you may very well find yourself under the guise of school pride
  singing a song... honoring a man and a past that fought to keep
  Black people enslaved at all cost.

You may see nothing wrong with a teenager graduating high
  school with a confederate general's name plastered on their
  diploma.
You will struggle with seeing the correlation between Jim Crow
  and mass incarceration, the 1963 16th Street Baptist Church
  bombing and the 2015 Charleston church massacre.
You will fail to see how privilege affords some with a high-quality
  education, and others the bare minimum.
You may not see a need to work to dismantle systems that have
  been the center of oppression
Because these topics are not taught in home and school lessons.

We cannot disregard a past that directly affects our present
  naively thinking it will not affect our future.

I've Heard. I've Seen. I've Witnessed.

Oh what Black eyes have seen.
Taken from home... forced across seas
Mother and brother killed, daughter and son stolen from hip,
    husband in field getting whipped.

Oh where Black feet have gone.
Treading troubled waters... running across pastures chasing
    freedom... till kingdom come.

Oh what Black ears have heard.
The cries, the prayers, the screams.

Oh what Black bodies have felt.
forced entry, the ripping of skin, the burning of flesh, lynched,
    beat, chained
But one thing Black people don't know is defeat.

Black people's names were stripped from them but now they find
    no rest in folks' mouths.
But now we conquer football fields, political races, bodies
    be our own,
we build homes and reside in them
we build schools and we learn in them
Black be what many would wish for again.
To be heir of soul-snatching music.
To birth greatness.
To birth nations.
To make a dollar out of 15 cents.
That's what Black people do.
We make nothing into something
that's the honest truth.

Juneteenth.

I heard some news finally made its way down to Texas.
It's hard to keep things "hush hush" when there's a message.
Let me tell you a little something about Juneteenth
Black people were never meant to be in chains!
We were always meant to be free!

They say this day commemorates the ending of slavery here in
the U.S.
Black people have been coming together for years to celebrate
our independence.

We be gathering in streets
Cookouts hosted in the country and the city
Parades where Black Queens sit on the top of cars,
crown on top of head, everybody getting fed.
A day full of Black Joy and throwing candy in front yards.
Music bumpin loud—in our big fancy cars.

Motorcycles flooding the streets
Laughter filling the air.
A celebration of liberation.
Living life with love and care.
Thinking oh what a day, oh what a dream
oh how many many years it took to get here.

What is Freedom??

When Freedom is not outside or in home.
Tell me, where does it reside?
What does it look like?
Who does it look like?

When you google the word freedom, it says "the power or right to
act, speak, or think as one wants without hindrance
or restraint."

By this definition, is freedom something out of reach for me?
Is it a privilege that the law protects when it's someone other
than me?

January 6.

Jaw dropped... but surprised is not the word.
I've heard and seen this before.
Temper tantrums normally lead to consequences.
They normally lead to teachable moments.
But you're the exception.
You've always been America's favorite child.

They gave you freedom.
Made way for opportunity.
Gave you bootstraps and a backpack.
Created systems so you have no setbacks.
They told you—you could run free in the world, at the grocery
    store, and now you've found your way to the capitol door.

You force your way in.
You break laws and some police officers help you downstairs.
Some take pictures that document the day's affairs.
You're applauded for your recklessness and your terroristic
    behavior is overlooked.
But you've always been America's favorite child.

Curfew.
You better be in by 6.
You take your time though—resting in assurance that you won't
    be escorted through a police door.
You go home.
You go to sleep.
What a privilege to believe you won't be held accountable for
    one thing.

Some will ask, when you wake up
look in the mirror—how do you not see thug or hypocrite?
You see American—you see patriot.
I tell them, it's because you've always been America's
    favorite child.

Newsroom.

Phone rings
Facebook messages are popping up
Everyone's asking the same question.
Why is Jeopardy not on?
Well ma'am, sir, right now there is a special report regarding the
   impeachment inquiry concerning the president.
I don't want to watch this.
I want to watch Jeopardy.
Well, ma'am, sir... some may argue that's the state the country is
   currently in.

Why does truth sting?

You know what I've learned?
Hate makes its way into schools, into churches,
into bars, by way of heart.
... by way of mind, fixed on the idea that a difference in religion,
    race, and opinion justifies senseless killings.
And who's to blame?
Individuals behind terroristic acts
or persons speaking life into death.

Or both?

Is it not true that premeditation comes by way of preparation?
The loading of more than one weapon
one physical... the other mental.
Bullets enter into gun by way of hand.
Bullets enter into mind by way of words—pacifying the
    insecurities of those who believe in some way they are
    being threatened.

Hate makes its way from the tip of one's tongue, to the entry of
one's mind, to the door of one's heart... through weakness...
through unrealistic fear
through the power struggle of one's self unable to cope with the
    fact that you are not the only person meant to be alive.

Must I?

Must I call out the injustices I see?
Must I scream?
Must I walk in streets?
Must I contact my representatives?
To remind them—to plead.
To convince them to act, to save, to protect the innocent.
Civilians
Being taken.
Being killed.
Being bombed.
Being left in a constant state of mourning.
Who will be to blame in the morning?
Who will get to see the morning?

Complicit is Decision.
Whether you're the one who yields the power
Or goes along with... keeping us in
a cycle of hate, of pain, of grief
Repeating history.

The belief that death brings peace... brings justice.
When it's freedom!
What do you do when everyone just wants their freedom?
When everyone just wants their freedom
Must I come to my neighbors, come to a stranger's aid?
So that their freedom is obtained?
Must I be the conscience
Of myself, my family, my friends, my community, my country.

I dare say I must be.

Why Vote? Why Bother?

Why bother to vote?
Well for some it ain't always been something we were able to do.
People were threatened and killed for this freedom we refuse
    to use.

We go back and forth on whether our ballot counts
When in truth, it's what democracy is all about.
You have a say on who represents you
You have a say on who's the right fit,
From school board, city, state and country, you determine who
    will sit,
In a place where their voice becomes the echo of your vote
You give your power away to those who actually show up to
    the polls.
Today you say this issue is none of your concern
But who's to say that it won't be during someone's 1–2-year term.

You may be saying, I want to vote but I don't know who to choose.
Well, you have to do your research... that's the only way a sound
    decision can be made.
Doing your best to know everyone's name on the ballot page.

What are the issues that affect you and the community in which
    you live?
How are laws affecting your money, your body, your livelihood
    and your kids?
What about your taxes, your health care, and the governmental
    programs designed to assist you?

What about your family members and friends who are troops?
You want to make sure they're under the guidance of a leader
who's capable and astute.

Your silence may one day leave you voiceless.
Your passiveness may one day leave you choice-less.
And regardless of this fact, someone that you love will always be
affected by you deciding not to act.

So, get up and register, do your research, and vote.
You ask why, it's simple.
Today you have a choice... what if tomorrow you don't?

The Cost.

We dare not think of the cost of it all.
Because it's not convenient?
Because folks don't care?
But I pray for the children who know pain, anger.
Who battle with forgiveness
Who contemplate vengeance.
I pray for the hearts broken, and hardened
By what they experience.
Generations traumatized
Cast aside
As if they be deserving.
And what does it mean to be deserving... who is deserving? Of
    pain... of trauma?

What is the cost?
Innocence being lost.
Peace never fully being in reach.
Pain... emptiness
A cycle.

Is it a determined heart?
That may or may not be fixed on someone one day paying
    the cost.
And don't we all in some way on some day, end up paying
    the cost?

{Insert Date, Month, Year}.

You know,
After the killing is done
And after some time has passed
Some will grow a conscience.

Activists will be quoted—
Maybe a museum will be built
Books will be written
And those who dream for political power will weave the dead's
   stories into their speeches.

They will expect but will not request forgiveness.
Though bearing witness
they will deem their words to be sufficient.

HONESTY

Court.

I feel like we've always been lawyers
You know, having to convince others, defending our humanity
And always ready to address
Harms inflicted
And having a self-appointed judge and jury who frequently refuse
  to listen
And then there is the prep before even getting into the room
The mental hula hoops we go through
Hair—check
Attire—check
Body language
And tone
Practicing how we handle objections in our mirrors at home
Anticipating it being sustained and precedent being repeatedly
  called on
Because folks like tradition
Folks like control
So even though you have the evidence and your case is strong
You're fighting through their belief that you don't belong
Having to suppress your emotions... even though everyone else in
  the room doesn't
Knowing that if you allow an ally to be first chair
You'd probably get a little farther than if they weren't there.
And with all the things you must consider
You still show up
Being witness and defender of self in a system that's corrupt.

Being Black.

I wonder if Michael heard about Trayvon
If Breonna heard about Atatiana and if Atatiana heard
   about Botham
I wonder if George heard about Eric and if Eric heard about Oscar
I wonder if Daunte heard about Philando and
if Philando heard about Sandra...
I wonder if Tamir heard about Rekia.

You see 9 times out of 10 they probably heard about the other
   because death makes Black people famous.
Our lives aren't cherished.
Our murderers are impulsive.
Meaning they act without forethought?
Meaning acting without justifiable consequence?

You do know that a bullet don't kill nobody's dream but the
   person in front of the trigger.
They say they fear they won't go home... they do,
ironically mistaking phone for gun, used by victim to call
   home too.

I wonder if my Black brothers and sisters thought the train
   was safe,
that a street was a public place,
that a car with family inside; equates to family time,
that a playground was the place to be,
I wonder if they thought that walking and standing in a
   neighborhood was in fact, no crime at all.

I wonder if they deemed home a sanctuary
that around the dinner table or couch they discussed the
injustices that came before them.

To be Black is to know that unmerited sufferings could one day
    be your own.
One day be part of your story.
That your name could one day be at the center of protest.
Your face plastered on tv screens and t-shirts.

It's crazy how the killer knows nothing about you, until you
    are gone.
They only know Black skin in the moment.
They only know they hold a gun... they hold a shield that covers
    their sins.

This is mine.

This is not a movie with multiple takes.
You cannot go into a place
And take it by force.
This territory is not yours.

And although this place may look familiar
It is mine!
This is home for me.
Where I unwind and deal with the joys and troubles of the day.
Unmerited suffering should never enter that doorway.

But...
You make your way in.
Why is it so hard to believe that this place is not yours?

NO!

My hands do not have to go up... surrendering in the home that I
    own is my choice.
I am not required to bend to your will... and attempt to pacify
    your fears.

"Please," does not have to come before the word leave.
Just leave!
I owe you nothing.
Leave.
And let me be
... leave me breathing.

Longevity.

What do we mean when we say we want Black folk to grow old?
Well... it really don't mean nothing too grand,
We just want our kids to graduate with a diploma in hand, and
　　degreed if they so choose.
We want to be able to make mistakes and learn from them
and after traffic stop—return home again.
We want legacy.
We want a child to know love from family.
We want freedom to not be a promise but a reality.
We want disagreement to be just that—no bringing out guns and
　　knives. No taking each other's lives.
We want healthy food joints around the block
And fresh produce always in stock
We want great health care
Opportunities in every field regardless of style of hair
In all, we want breath for years to come
We want a great quality of life.
One that is ours. And one that is not cut short.

Change is coming.

When people are trying to understand my people.
I tell them, you have to go to the past.
You have to go all the way back... across the Atlantic.
Back to when my people were stolen and taken captive and
thrown below deck.

I tell them, you would have to have a conversation with the sharks
back then to ask them... how often they feasted... and how they
grew to know African blood so well.
I tell them that death followed them from sea to land.
That they were chained like animals, then sold as property,
separated from their family and deemed everything but human.

You see human, meant white.
It meant European, it meant right.
It meant, your right to life.
Black meant beast.
It meant African.
It meant your life was nothing but a piece of capital.
Your life was at your master's disposal.

I tell them that melanin got you discriminated against in the north
and got you killed down south.
Got your Wall Street burned down.
Got you beat in Alabama.
Got you lynched in Mississippi.

I tell them that melanin ain't never been seen as friendly.
We have always been seen as a threat... as suspect.

I will tell them... that if you want to understand my people, you
   have to know that there is a cause and effect.
And when a race has seen so much death... it is not your place to
   tell them how to cope... to tell them how to feel.
To tell them that their stories are only valid when they're coming
   from a white storyteller.

Can we tell our stories, and you still listen?
Because I will tell you how my people are resilient.
How we learned how to wade in the water, cuz we wasn't gonna
   let nobody turn us around.
You see, we knew change was coming.
And to understand my people, you have to know that change is
   always coming!

Black History.

When I think of Black history,
I think of Carter G. Woodson, Fannie Lou Hamer,
    Shirley Chisholm.
I think of the years before 1619.
I think of 1619.
I think of auction blocks.
I think of lynch parties.

I think of Harriet and her northern star.
I think of Mahalia Jackson daring Martin to speak of his dream.
I think of Claudette Colvin refusing to give up her seat.
I think of Colin Kaepernick refusing to stand to his feet.

I think of Maxine Waters reclaiming her time.
I think of Jackie Robinson, when the Dodgers wanted him to sign.
I think of LeBron James following through with his promises.
I think of Barack Obama in the presidential office.

I think of a time when Black people were merely entertainment.
The history of caricatures and blackface.

I think of Whitney's voice—Beyoncé's passion,
I think of Black comedians that keep us laughing.
I think of Angela Rye speaking the truth.
I think of Tiffany Dena Loftin mobilizing the youth.
I think of Emmett Till and the Central Park 5.
I think of Hattie McDaniel, Gabrielle Douglas and Simone Biles.
I think of the ironing board, the traffic light, and GPS.
I think of the Black Lives Matter movement and every
    Black activist.
I think of SNCC, NAACP, and the Black Panther Party.
I think of the first time I ever saw a Black barbie.

I think of Serena and tennis.
I think of Black artists, Black poets, and Black politicians.
I think of Tyler Perry and his journey to ownership.
I think of HBCUs, the Divine 9 and Toni Morrison.
I think of Sojourner Truth's, "ain't I a woman?"
And Michelle Obama, and the power of becoming.
I think of OWN and BET
I think of Kamala Harris, yes, madam VP.

When I think of Black history, I think of me.
I think of every Black boy and Black girl who has pushed and is
    pushing to be... EVERYTHING our ancestors dared to dream.

Unnamed.

No one told me about you.
I didn't read about you in a textbook
Your name was never mentioned in the classroom.
Not even at the Black history bowl.
But I guess... you don't know what you don't know.

But I know you existed.

Say it's something in my spirit—a feeling.
You may not have been on the front lines, but you were there.
Maybe not giving speeches to the masses,
But maybe helping with staffing
organizing, planning, making phone calls, spreading the
    message... keeping records.
Maybe you were watching over other folks' families,
helping folks become educated
as teacher or researcher,
maybe you patched up wounds, prepared food
Served up encouragement and prayed through disappointment.
Maybe you were bodyguard, watchman,
Maybe you were the person before the person with the well-
    known name,
Maybe you laid the groundwork for the person we know as the
    "first" came.
Maybe you rioted and fought
Maybe you were the one they caught
Maybe you were the one who entertained, who danced, who sung,
    who drew,
Maybe you were the one who built, who drove, who knew—that
    you would not be in the history books

Your role wouldn't garner the world's attention
That your name wouldn't be one that folks would know
   or mention.

But you existed!

And I don't need a photo to know that.
I don't need anyone to tell me that.

Without a shadow of a doubt progress was made,
Due to the efforts of my ancestors who go unnamed.

Teach Me.

Just so you know.
I am not in that percentage of kids you automatically think—drops
    out of school and heads directly to the streets.
No.
You will not catch me doing that classic nod—drive by—
    handshake—money and narcotics trade—that is not me.
And contrary to your belief—I actually have a desire to go to
    school and get an education.
but you see the problem is when—the condition of the school that
    I attend is determined by the neighborhood in which it is in.
When I am expected to learn in an environment that isn't even
    suitable enough to be taught in.
You see, the problem is when, my teachers already have
    preconceived notions on the rate in which I will learn because
    they think—that kids in my social class cannot retain
    information as quickly as other kids that attend school in the
    wealthier part of the city.
Therefore, I am not challenged.
I am not challenged because they see very little potential in
    someone like me.
And they won't say this verbally, but it becomes evident when
    they teach, and I know this because I've sat—I've sat through
    mediocre lectures.
Not blind to the fact that they try to dim down the material
    because they don't think that I can comprehend it all.
So, they refuse to give me books filled with philosophical
    meaning and historical readings because they assume I'm
    already dealing with problems at home—and they don't want to
    give me a heavier load.
And in their eyes... they are helping me.
But what they don't realize is that they are crippling me—making
    me dependent on them—they may or may not be purposely
    producing lower class citizens.

But this is not okay with me and regardless of what you think of me... my destiny is not tied to being in prison or on the street.

I was told that the key to a better life is an education—so give me the opportunity to obtain it.
Teach me.
Do not rob me of my education.

Teach me about my history—and do not assign it to just one week in February.
And in that time—do not intertwine fabricated lies to make my country seem pretty.
Do not filter the truth.
Because history is living proof of how mistakes can be made but how we as a country can overcome difficult times and reach better days.
Teach me about how Sally had two apples and had three mouths to feed and how difficult that would be with a person who could not bring home a consistent salary.
Teach me about Chemistry—how nations can disagree but there is a way for us to live in harmony.
Teach me about the beauty of every language—the power of the spoken word.
Teach me about how every positive change that has occurred was because the youth demanded their voices to be heard.

Teach me!
Because I have a desire to learn.

And you may have to add to your role because my generation may not be receiving what we need from home—so you may have to teach him how to be a man and teach her how to be a woman.
Because the only way we can successfully lead is if you teach.
So, teach.
TEACH ME.

Kiddos.

It's crazy how children have to fight for their lives and fight for
the truth in the classroom.
They're having sit-ins and walkouts... trying to bring
change about
And some adults are refusing to listen...
Acting like their voices, stories, concerns, and demands, aren't
worthy of their attention.
But the young are relentless—they know they have power and
they will use it.
Rejecting all excuses
because they are tired of thoughts and prayers... brace
yourselves... for the next time
Because the next time—always seems to come.
But here they come
the young folks
The leaders of today and tomorrow.

Processing the day.

It's 5am
and I'm up… thinking about how yesterday I had more rights than
    I do today.
The fact that there is someone else who has the "power" to
    determine what I can and cannot do with my body, baffles me.
And at the same time some government folks are proposing to
    pay us to have a baby.
Now that's crazy.

But now it's 7am and I gots to go to work.
I gots to get to this money,
cuz groceries ain't cheap.
And you know what, everyday somebody tries to gaslight me—
saying that the price of eggs ain't gone up
So, I show them the receipts.
You should see the way they look at me as they try to conjure up
    some reasoning that feeds their own beliefs.

But I move the conversation along because it's 9am
and there's a lot of other things going on.
Like is it safe to drink the milk and eat the chicken?
Because chileee listen
a lot of folks are getting fired.
Many federal workers are getting laid off the job.
So, who's doing the safety checks?
Are they even happening?

It's 11am
And my group chat is silent.
Meanwhile some government officials are inviting civilians to
    signal chats and are wildin.
Are folks safe?

It's 1pm
And a teacher's contract wasn't renewed after she called her
    student by their preferred name.

You would think folks would be focused on how literacy rates
    keep going down
but the younger generation isn't a group that people really seem
    to care about.

It's 3pm now
and there is an attack on museums—on history as a whole.
Unfortunately, it's not surprising though.

It's 5pm
and I'm trying to figure out my role in the movement.
Thinking if someone could just tell me what to do, I will do it.

It's 7pm
I'm trying to work out—then I find out students are getting taken
off the streets because they exercised their first amendment right.
And there is also this false narrative around DEI (Diversity,
    Equity, and Inclusion).

It's 9pm
social media got me by my chinny chin chin
It seems like some people are living their best lives while others
    are occasionally talking about what's going on in the country...
    in the world
But if you scroll for a little bit... it's like reality doesn't exist.
Or it's being intentionally manipulated.
Keeping one overwhelmed and overstimulated.

It's 11pm
It's time to go to sleep.
So, I try to meditate
in an effort to keep my worries at bay.
I don't want them to follow me in my dreams.
This is me... in a constant state of processing.

Baby, this world is cruel.

A woman is weeping for her unborn child.
She says, "Do you know what I fear most about this pregnancy?
It is the fact that, beyond the womb lies uncertainty.
I cannot guarantee my child's safety, I'm trying to figure out ways
     to say, baby, this world is cruel.
I do not know if you are safe at school; maybe I should just keep
     you home.
Because I have formulated reoccurring images in my mind, of the
     tragedies in Pakistan, Sandy Hook, and Columbine, and I am
     afraid of losing you."

A woman of the Muslim faith is weeping for her unborn child.
And when this same question is asked, she says, "I am afraid that
     my child will be harassed.
When 'random searches' at the airport soon become routine.
Interrogating my child as if they have a means to cause harm,
     because someone with the same hue as them decided to make
     9/11 a date to remember.
Having to constantly remind my child, it is not your fault that you
     remind them of September. And my child will ask, 'لماذا انا,' why
     me? And I will respond يا حبيبتي هذا العالم قاسي,' baby, this world is
     cruel. They would have preferred that you remained naked
     when exiting my womb, but I covered your head."

There is a woman weeping for her unborn child.
She says, "They will say that my child doesn't belong.
That this land that we immigrated to, is not their home.
They will respect the ancestry of our food, call it Mexican.
But refuse to call us by our names instead, illegal aliens.
And my child will ask, 'Por qué yo?' Why me? And I will say, 'bebé
     este mundo es cruel!' Baby, this world is cruel.
We live in a place where they refer to themselves as a melting pot;
     but it's you they try to exclude."

There is a woman weeping for her unborn child.
She is afraid that a tombstone will know her child's name well
before a diploma.
She says, "My child will constantly be looking over their shoulder,
no hoodie will see the inside of their closet, they will be
constantly reminded that ghosts are what they make of our
people.
The system, is anticipating their arrival and as soon as my
umbilical cord is cut, they will have entered into a war well
before they are one and my child will ask, 'Why me' and I will
say 'baby, this world is cruel. You will have to learn to love your
skin while living in a world where they categorize and
marginalize people of your pigment."

But baby, be strong.
You have more allies than you can possibly imagine.
Walls may be built but love will always find a way to seep
through.
And yes, "baby, this world is cruel, but I will do my very best to
protect you!"

Doing the devil's work.

Last night a mother spoke to her child one last time.
Last night, a grandmother prayed that her baby would return
  home safe.
Last night, that baby was having a good time.

Until, 3, 2, 1.
Dancing turned into ducking and running.
Fun turned into fear and chaos.
Life turned into death within a matter of minutes, within seconds.
Two people full of purpose were taken.
They're lives—stolen.

How dare you come and put a timer on their breath!
How dare you come and strip them of their steady heartbeat!
How dare you turn a joyous night into a dreadful one!
How dare you come and do the devil's work and ride off into the
  wind while strangers hold the bodies of other people's friends.
How dare you turn celebration into mourning!

Young.

I don't think we talk about it enough.
How death is something that youth experience.
How one's life has really just begun and then it suddenly ends.
It's rough—to grieve the young.
It's heavy.
How unfair it seems that they gave so much light to this world for
   but a moment.

HUMANITY

Grace.

As soon as the plane landed
And we heard that *ding* to unbuckle our seat belts
He got up
Rushed to the front
Some folks were mad and made snarky remarks as he passed
Others laughed at what was said
But no one stopped to consider
If he had a connecting flight and if he couldn't afford to miss it.

Little did they know he didn't have time to explain his intention
  because he was on his way to say his last goodbye... to someone
  he has loved all his life.

She was driving a little slower than most
So, folks honked their horns
Hoping it would move her along
It didn't
She kept her pace
The honking continued as people drove by with their irritation
  visibly on their faces.
But she kept her eyes on the road.

Little did they know she had recently witnessed a tragic
  car accident
And she couldn't stop replaying it in her mind, so she pays close
  attention to every road sign
she's locked in and moves with extreme caution.
This is her way of keeping folks safe while she's making her way
  down the highway.

They came to work without a smile
And that didn't go over too well with their customers
You see, they expected to receive their order from a server that
  had a bit more energy
That interacted with their table a bit more frequently
  and gleefully.

So, they complained

Wanting to speak to their manager... they asked for their name.

Little did they know that they were going through some things
    and it was affecting them greatly
So, mustering up someone else's preferred level of energy... was a
    lot to expect when
they were already giving all they had left.

Remember that our paths may cross but the life we walk
    is individual.
And you never know what someone is going through.
Folks have reasons that you may not be privy to.
So, extend grace.
And when you need it. I pray you receive it.

Interactions.

I had a random conversation with a stranger at a book fair... then
   another in a rideshare... then at the farmers market... and then
   at a dope little restaurant.

To be honest, there were times when I wanted to talk and other
   times I did not—but I engaged with each stranger anyway.

And each interaction was a reminder that we're all trying
   our best.

And that it's nice to talk to somebody... even if it's someone you
   do not know.
You may find yourself being a little vulnerable... while you both
   unintentionally help one another connect the dots... as y'all
   attempt to clear your heads of a myriad of thoughts.

Or maybe you just come across someone who is effortlessly kind.

They ask you how you're doing, and they stay to hear your
   response instead of just casually carrying on.
It's refreshing to be seen and to engage with someone who is
   intentionally listening.

And when you transition to the next topic,
you both realize you have a few things in common.
And as the conversation comes to an end and you prepare to go
   your separate ways
You find that your day is a little better
you feel a little lighter
And it's all due to a stranger you will probably never meet again.

There is something truly beautiful about these social interactions.

Acts of Kindness.

When disaster hits,
And reality shifts,
You hope that folks will show up—that help will come.

And right now, there are people choosing each other.
Lending their bodies,
Risking their lives,
Volunteering their time,
And giving what they have to both neighbor and stranger.

A text, a phone call, a voice message—sent.
A hug, some funds, we see love in action.

Empathy and care are on full display.

It reminds me, that in times of crisis—much is lost.
But the very best part of humanity is not.

Foreshadowing.

I'm anticipating the day
When my child will read books
That were placed in their hands by my hands
Regardless of said book bans
And they will ask me...
With so much compassion in their heart
Is death by the hands of any man necessary or justified?
And I will start by saying it depends on who you ask.
If you are a victim by truth—wanting freedom—you may deem
    it necessary.
If you are a victim by illusion—you may deem it justified
On the topic of slavery, apartheid, genocide,
They will say Ma, there is clearly a right and a wrong side
Like a good guy and bad guy
But why?
Why were people treated less than
Why must freedom be a privilege
Why didn't folks stop them
And I'll say....

Sometime silence is paid for
And calculated
Financed like war
Baby, folks like their comfort
Even if it sometimes comes by way of the death and/or control
    of another
They'll say...
Well maybe some folks didn't know
Maybe death and truth are things their algorithms didn't show.
I'm sure if people knew, they would do something
And I'll say... baby, if you're not careful that expectation can lead
    to disappointment

But, "Ma, how can someone just turn a blind eye?"

I'll say, unfortunately it's something that humans do all the time
I think it's fear of losing something, like comfort, friends, a job
 offer, political office, power... there could be many reasons

"Well, Ma... speaking up and standing on what's right would be
 my decision.

Because everyone deserves their freedom

In my own way I would do my part
I would help
there is no question
In my own way I would step in, step up, speak up,

Because it's only right... it's only right, Ma."

Courage.

I think I got a little fight in me.
Got that courage Ms. Angelou talked about... that's needed to
　　practice all other virtues consistently.
I got a little—we shall not be moved
That boycott type energy.
I got that—you ain't heard from me in a minute
But clock it, I done got my rest.
This next part... I do not say in jest!
You can mess around and find out.
This lineage you may not know nothin about
because they don't teach it
But my ancestors made sure we knew freedom.
So, I'd be dang if we only experience a few decades of progress.
We won't regress.
We will keep pushing.
You'll see,
Like I said, I got a little fight in me.

To those who choose to teach.

You know they say that education is the key to a better life
The key to success, to freedom, to the future
And you hold that key in your hands
Your ability to unlock the potential that we all possess
You spark curiosity, interest, purpose,
Creating space for our cognitive development
Making learning fun and relevant
You go above and beyond
You are a keeper of young, of old, of community, of nations
    as a whole
You are a home away from home
You are mentor
Confidant
You are part of the village who raises the child
To be informed, to be self-aware, a problem solver, an innovator,
    a sense maker,
You are influencer
To the young
Helping them see the world, and understand it... encouraging
    them to make it... a better place
You are the place where a child's dreams can be fueled
You may be their genesis
Of discovering who they are
What role they are meant to play
You stretch their minds day after day.
You equip them with the tools they will use well beyond the walls
    of any school
Your job is no walk in the park... it takes heart, passion,
    skill, perseverance.
You make the difference.
Thank you for choosing to teach
For being what this world will always need.

Trust.

I was driving across a bridge the other day
And I thought about the hands, the bodies, the minds responsible
   for its existence
I thought about those who tend to its needs
To ensure it maintains the ability to serve its purpose.
How a bridge was once an answer to a desire... to a problem... to a
   dream that one could not yet fathom
And since its inception, it continues to be a connector
   of destinations.
I start thinking about how we trust its design,
And drive, and ride, and walk, and run... across it
Believing it will withstand the weight and the conditions that were
   considered before and during its build
I thought about how some of us get up and crossover a man-made
   bridge every day.
A bridge created by strangers.
But we trust what they've created.
With our lives
We trust the hands, the bodies, the minds responsible for
   its existence.
We trust they got it right.
So, we drive... and we make our way to the other side.

Rideshare.

To the uber driver who turned his head and said to me,
"Gosh, you're beautiful..."
To which I replied: "Thank you."

When you said what you said
A lot of thoughts started swirling in my head
Like how kind of you
To verbalize to me that you see beauty when you look at me
But then I start thinking about my safety
How that statement may have been a little bit too bold for
    my liking.

Then I wonder whether I'm making this out to be
more than what it is—am I being extra, dramatic, paranoid for
    no reason?
But unfortunately... one can never be too sure
Because the reality is, I'm in your car, so by default I'm not
    100 percent... secure.

And then you start asking me questions
Trying to make conversation
Asking, what do I do? Am I from here? How long have I
    been here?
I try to be short with my reply, yet kind
But truthfully my answers are not sincere
Because I don't know you
And all these thoughts are swirling in my head
Based on other people's experiences and the reality in which girls
    all over the world find themselves

So, I share my location with my friend.
I double check that my seat belt can unbuckle, and I
    buckle it again.
I roll down my window
I place my fingers on the two buttons on the side of my phone
And pray that I get to my destination safely.

In which I did.

So, to the uber driver who turned his head and said to me
"Gosh, you're beautiful..."
Thank you for getting me to where I needed to be.
For as you can see, it was truly a journey for me.

There is a stranger somewhere...

Making sure that the stop lights work, that the roads are safe, that the bridges are maintained.

There is a stranger somewhere tending to the power lines after a storm and standing by ready to support.

There is a stranger somewhere
Waking up at the crack of dawn
Planting, harvesting, managing crops—they are the reason stores and markets have food in stock.

There is a stranger somewhere
Studying the human anatomy—so they can properly diagnose and treat and save a life if need be.

There is a stranger somewhere
driving up—making sure the mail arrives, and garbage gets picked up.

There is a stranger somewhere filling potholes in the streets and working on the sewer pipes—in an effort to keep folks safe.

There is a stranger somewhere keeping people informed and/or entertained.

There is a stranger somewhere working behind the scenes lending their expertise.

There is a stranger somewhere... ready to come to our aid.
... helping us get to point A and point B
... by bus, by train, by car, by airplane

There is a stranger somewhere keeping buildings, houses, and
    cities clean
... jumping at the opportunity to give back to their community.

So, when cynicism tries to show its face and temptations arise to
    lean into hate
Remember there is a stranger somewhere contributing to your
    life in some way.
Every day.
Even if they go unnoticed
There is a stranger somewhere...

Anticipation.

If my child asks me one day
What do you love about humanity?
I will say,
The kindness that I've experienced and witnessed
The thoughtful gesture of a stranger to someone in need of
    their assistance

I love when we intentionally listen
And when our resolve is strengthened
I love when we learn from our mistakes
When we build, when we create, and make a way for each other's
    lifetimes to be better
I love when we communicate—in logic, in reason, with emotion,
    in the language that our great grandmother speaks
I love how empathy can transform us
How we make home in another's body before we make
    introduction to the rest of the world.
I love that when we choose to be—we are a safe place
    for somebody.
We are confidant, supporter, collaborator, accountability partner.
I love when we look out for each other.
And want the best for one another.
That's what I love.
When human beings choose to act with love.

Hope.

When I think of hope.
I think of James Baldwin
When he penned a letter saying, "we can make America what it
    must become."
The audacity of this man,
Using words such as Can and Must.
Declaring that we are both capable and responsible... for what's
    to come.

Hope be the words of Dr. Maya Angelou
Rising in spite of circumstance,
Hope be the dream that is not deferred.
One that Langston would not question.
It's a word that would be woven into Dr. King's Sunday lessons.

A 4-letter word that keeps us reaching, for better and for more.

Hope—a word that requires belief... that something worthy is
    awaiting us—that something better is in store.

Oh hope...
Is what keeps us holding on... weaved in a prayer that it won't
    be long.

Yes, hope can inspire movements and imagination.
Hope...
A word that must be for what we aim—the anticipation
    for celebration.

I know hope be a word we cling to.
One that we hope will be enough.
Being a hopefully hopeful optimistic
Can be tiring and tough
But one thing is for sure.
One thing is for certain
Hope and work get us closer to our destination... for both serve
    a purpose.

Accountability.

Whatever awaits...
We must attach our names to it
For that be the legacy in which we leave behind
Good or bad
Choices were made
And our collective reality becomes what we allow, what we settle
    for, what we intentionally work toward
For I reckon, we all have a say in the present

All in last night's dream.

Last night I had a dream that there was no such thing as broken.
    whether that be heart, family, or country.
I saw hearts whole... with no holes.
        no space for hate nor pain to reside.
I saw parents... present
        and active in a child's life.
I saw a stranger comfortable in their skin.
I saw family not worried of deportation.
I saw Black bodies coming out of the ground in which they were
    placed too soon.
            I walked outside to blue skies and clean air.
Pollution was not a thing.
I saw humans being loving mortals
        All in last night's dream.

Why do you write?

They ask, "why do you write?"
I tell them, it is space in which I can be free... I can be me.
It is where pain, joy, and everything in between can live on
  paper... at the same time.
It is my attempt to confront the truth.
It is where my healing begins.

God made tree that was turned into paper.
God made man that made pen and tech.
God made me.
God gave me words.
God gave me a voice.
God gave me courage.
God, thank you for providing me with everything I need
    to tell story.

---Love, Nytesia Ross

Acknowledgements.

To the woman who raised me, you are all types of worthy.
You are worthy of everything good.
Momma, thank you for your sacrifice and your love.
You have always been an artist.
I am amazed at your ability to pick up pieces and make a
    masterpiece, every single time.
I love you.
Thank you for loving me and believing in me.
Thank you for always allowing me to be an open book.

To the woman whose life lessons never leave my tongue,
    you are appreciated.
Granny, thank you for being a fountain of wisdom.
You are a person of love and truth.
You are an inspiration. You are backbone.
Thank you for answering my phone calls, no matter the hour.
Thank you for loving me and being my PIC.

Once upon a time, a young Black girl... wanted to write a poetry book of her own. Today, this Black woman made it happen.

"Never give up on your dreams... never give up on you."
-Nytesia Ross

About the Author

Nytesia Ross is passionate about the power of stories and the people behind them, dedicating her life to both. An award-winning poet, she has performed on renowned stages across the country—from New York to California—and at the prestigious Kennedy Center in Washington, D.C. Her work has been featured on NPR's All Things Considered podcast, as well as at Stanford's World House Documentary Film Festival. Beyond poetry, Nytesia is an accomplished videographer whose work has been recognized by the Association for the Study of African American Life and History. She is a proud member of Alpha Kappa Alpha Sorority, Incorporated® and lives by the words of Philippians 4:13: "I can do all things through Christ who strengthens me."

www.ingramcontent.com/pod-product-compliance
Lightning Source LLC
Chambersburg PA
CBHW021204130626
46554CB00005B/1973